The Bodies Beneath the Table

Adastra Press Publications of W. D. Ehrhart

Nuclear Quartet 1980 (broadsheet w/ Merritt Clifton,
    Gary Metras & Miriam Sagan)
Matters of the Heart 1981
The Outer Banks & Other Poems 1984
Winter Bells 1988
The Distance We Travel 1993
Mostly Nothing Happens 1995
Beautiful Wreckage: New & Selected Poems 1999
Gifts 2003 (broadside)
Sleeping with the Dead 2006
The Bodies Beneath the Table 2010

The Bodies Beneath the Table

W. D. Ehrhart

Adastra Press
Easthampton

Copyright © 2010 by W. D. Ehrhart

First Edition

ISBN 10: 0-9822495-7-8
ISBN 13: 978-0-9822495-7-4

Some of these poems have previously appeared in *American Poetry Review*, *Asha*, *Big Hammer*, *Big Sky Journal*, *Bucks County Writer*, *Cimarron Review*, *Deadly Writers Patrol*, *Epoch Poetry Quarterly* (Taiwan), *Great River Review*, *Interchange* (UK), *Iraq Notebook / Cuaderno de Irak*, *Kurungabaa* (AUS), *Lummox Journal*, *Mad Poets Review*, *Michigan Quarterly Review*, *New Hampshire Gazette*, *New Letters*, *North American Review*, *Poetry Wales* (UK), *Rattle*, *River Poets Journal*, *San Pedro River Review*, *Schuylkill Valley Journal*, *South Boston Literary Gazette*, *Virginia Quarterly Review*, *VFP National Newsletter*, *Vooys* (NL), *VVAW Veteran*, *WLA (War, Literature & the Arts)*, *Zeitschrift für Australienstudien* (AUT), 48th Street Press Broadsides, Friday's Egg Calendar Company, and the limited edition chapbook *Sleeping with the Dead*, Adastra Press.

Library of Congress Control Number: 2010910298

Book design by Gary Metras in Garamond 12/15

Cover painting: *Red Table*, by Jane Irish, watercolor on paper, 8" x 11", 2007

Author photo by Linda Walters Photography

Adastra Press
16 Reservation Road
Easthampton, MA 01027

For Anne,
the love of my life

&

for Leela,
the other love of my life

Contents

I. Secret Lives

 What Better Way to Begin ... 11
 Burning Leaves ... 12
 Reading Out Loud ... 13
 The Secret Lives of Boys ... 14
 The Damage We Do ... 16
 Christmas Miracles ... 18
 Sins of the Fathers ... 19
 Music Lessons ... 20

II. Gravestones

 All About Death ... 23
 Gravestones at Oxwich Bay ... 24
 Redipuglia ... 25
 Home Before Morning ... 28
 Seminar on the Nature of Reality ... 30
 What Makes a Man ... 32
 Letting Go ... 34
 The Orphan ... 36

III. Extras

 The Wreckage Along the Road ... 39
 Meditations on Pedagogy ... 40
 Artsy Fartsy, Whiskey & Girls ... 42
 All About Love ... 43
 Oh, Canada ... 44
 What the Fuss Is All About ... 46
 Extra! Extra! ... 47
 Life in the Neighborhood ... 48

IV. Epiphanies

    Golfing with My Father ... 51
    Breakfast with You and Emily Dickinson ... 53
    Sleeping with the Dead ... 56
    Small Talk ... 57
    Children of Adam & Eve ... 58
    The Work of Love ... 59
    The Bombing of Afghanistan ... 60
    Epiphany ... 62

V. Bodies

    On the Eve of Destruction ... 65
    The Bodies Beneath the Table ... 67
    Kosovo ... 68
    September 11th ... 70
    Down and Out in Darfur ... 73
    Coaching Winter Track in Time of War ... 74
    Manning the Walls ... 75
    Turning Sixty ... 78

VI. One Hand Clapping

    Temple Poem ... 83

I. Secret Lives

What Better Way to Begin

You can just keep your rockets' red glare.
And as for the bombs bursting in air,
with all that noise and fire and smoke
there has to be plenty of jagged steel
looking for someone to hit.
Ask Gaffney with his shattered knee.
Ask Ski with a hole behind his ear
the size of a fist.
So I'm not too keen on fireworks.
Call it ghosts from the past.

But it's Millennium Eve
and my daughter wants to see the biggest
fireworks show the City of Philadelphia
has ever put on—or ever will—
in my lifetime or hers.
So off we go to join the crowd
on the banks of the Delaware River.

When midnight arrives, the crowd explodes
as the barges moored in the river
open fire in a steadily rising rumble
of thumps and sparks like four-deuce mortars.
But before the first bomb bursts in air,
Leela silently takes my hand
and holds it tight through the rockets' red glare
till the last bomb's blunt concussion
fades away as if it never were.

Burning Leaves

Something you just don't smell anymore:
burning leaves. Rake them into the street
and set them on fire. That was the way
we used to get rid of them. That was the way
you knew it was autumn. Football season.

Friday night, and the whole small town,
the young and the old and the in-between,
cousins and aunts and greats and grands,
the high school band and the cheerleading squad
packed into Poppy Yoder Stadium,

even the hoods and the rebels without a cause
under the stands in the shadows
smoking Winston and Kool,

out on the field, under the lights,
the hometown boys, the Pennridge Rams,
in victory or defeat, warrior heroes.

Then the long walk home beneath the stars,
the smell of burning leaves in the knife-
edged air of October, even the Milky Way
still visible, then, when I was a kid.

There must be something I can't remember.
It wasn't that way. It wasn't a Norman
Rockwell painting: boy with a banged-up knee
and a kindly cop seeing him safely home.
But things like that really happened.

Now-days, burn your leaves in the street,
cops show up and threaten to take you away.

Reading Out Loud

I hated it. That inescapable
moment each day my turn would come
and I would have no choice except to read
what David, Karen, Jimmy and Suzanne
read as if they were sliding on glass,
not crashing through it, lurching, stumbling,
every step a public demonstration
of stupidity, each sentence hours,
the teacher's cardboard smile and tapping foot,
rustling in the chairs around me, giggles
of the other kids Miss Connie used
to punish me, pretending not to hear.

The Secret Lives of Boys

Nothing the boy wanted
ever came true. Not the chance
to be a World War Two fighter ace
in 1958. Not the chance to save
beautiful Ursula Netcher
from pirates. Not the ability
to leap tall buildings
in a single bound.

Okay, he got that plastic
tripod-mounted battery-powered
machinegun for Christmas one year,
but it broke two days later.

And he got to pick the football helmet
with the plexiglass face mask
for selling the most
YMCA oatmeal cookies,
but it didn't make him
any better at football.

He got the job
handing out skates and changing records
on Sunday afternoons at the roller rink.

But he never got the things
that really mattered.
The courage to defend himself
from the playground bullies.
Parents who didn't show
one face to the world,

another inside the home.
The chance not to be the preacher's kid
in a town where you couldn't hide.

He got the double chin.
He got C's in gym class.
He got his brothers' hand-me-down clothes.

He wanted to be a Wildcat pilot,
or maybe a ball turret gunner.

He wanted to rescue beautiful Pam Magee
from pirates. Or maybe Comanches.

He wanted to be
anything
but what he was.

The Damage We Do

I don't know why I fell asleep
when I was eight at the top of the stairs
listening to my parents argue. Maybe I
thought they'd find me asleep and feel
so bad they'd learn how to get along.

I don't know why I put my fist
through the kitchen storm door glass
storming out of the house when I was ten,
but my mother had to wrap my hand
in a towel and call the doctor.
An accident, she said.

I don't know why I ran from the house
in my bare feet in February,
my father swearing, me in tears
and no clear thought but getting as far
away as a thirteen-year-old could get,
which wasn't far in a small town
where your dad's a minister, everyone
thinks he's a saint, and you're a disgrace
to be acting up the way you always do.

I don't remember a time when the house
I grew up in wasn't crackling with rage.
I don't know why. I think my father
was really a mess, but he didn't
discuss that with me, and my mother
just put up with him year after year.
You get so wired, you learn to think
that's the way life's supposed to be.

And you learn to be angry all the time.
You run away to California.
You join the Marines at seventeen.
You quit every job you don't get fired from.
After awhile you don't get hired,
and people avoid you; they think you're
out of control, and you probably are,
but it takes you most of a lifetime just
to begin to make the connections.

By then you've got a child of your own
who's angry all the time. I'd like to say
I don't know why, but I do.
I'd like to explain that it's not her fault,
but what's she supposed to do with that?
I'd like to undo the damage I've done,
but I don't know how.

Christmas Miracles

Leaving the party she takes my hand,
slips on icy sidewalk, squeezes
my hand to steady herself, laughs
a child's laugh. She tells me she hopes
I'll like the present she's made.
She imagines the presents she'll get.

Hand in hand we go through crackling
cold December night, her voice so bright
like moonlight on a field of snow,
so happy. As if she's forgotten
how scary an angry father can be,
how scary the brooding silences.

But tonight I'm a man who knows
what he's got. And tonight is Christmas Eve:
presents are waiting beneath the tree,
each one to my daughter a dream,
a desire, a wish, a new beginning.
Tonight she takes her father's hand
like a child who's not afraid.

Sins of the Fathers

Today my child came home from school in tears.
A classmate taunted her about her clothes,
and other kids joined in, enough of them
to make her feel as if the fault was hers,
as if she can't fit in no matter what.
A decent child, lovely, bright, considerate.
It breaks my heart. It makes me want someone
to pay. It makes me think—O Christ, it makes
me think of things I haven't thought about
in years. How we nicknamed Barbara Hoffman
"Barn," walked behind her through the halls and mooed
like cows. We kept this up for years, and not
for any reason I could tell you now
or even then except that it was fun.
Or seemed like fun. The nights that Barbara
must have cried herself to sleep, the days
she must have dreaded getting up for school.
Or Suzanne Heider. We called her "Spider."
And we were certain Gareth Schultz was queer
and let him know it. Now there's nothing I
can do but stand outside my daughter's door
listening to her cry herself to sleep.

Music Lessons

Standing where the water tumbles
down the broken beaver dam
above the old stone wall where
daffodils on slender stalks
nod beneath a seamless sky,
my daughter says, "Listen, Dad,
the creek is singing."

No use pointing out to her
the image isn't fresh.

How much she is her father's child;
how often adolescent need
to differentiate herself from me
becomes two stubborn people
butting heads.

But not today.

I'd have to be a fool to choose
this moment to instruct her
in the art of words.

And anyway, only the dead
at heart would ever argue
what we're hearing isn't
just exactly
what my daughter says it is.

II. Gravestones

All About Death

You don't want me to tell you about death,
but I'm going to tell you anyway:
it smells bad. It gets into your nostrils
and just sits there, stinking up everything.
It won't go away. Death creeps up on you
when you're least expecting it, even when
you can see it coming a mile away,
and rips your heart out through your throat and leaves
an empty place in your life you can't fill
with memories or exercise or wads
of sterile gauze, and walks away laughing.
Or maybe just slips out under the door
and floats away like mist dissipating
before sunlight on an autumn morning.
Death minds its own business and everyone
else's, too. Death does a little jig,
then lobs a grenade into your kitchen,
but it's only a dud. What a joker,
you think, just before it explodes. Death feels
sorry for nothing and no one. Death feels
nothing at all. Death drives an SUV
with a husband and two kids in Gladwyne,
loses control, crosses the median,
plows head-on into everyone sooner
or later, takes out a mortgage and then
skips town without paying a penny back.
Death takes a holiday, but not today.
Not tomorrow, either. Maybe next week,
but don't bank on it. My mother-in-law
died twenty-five years ago, but my wife
still cries out in her sleep for her mommy.
Sometimes my wife isn't even asleep.

Gravestones at Oxwich Bay

St. Iltyd's Church
Gower, Wales

I.

"When the archangel's trump shall sound
And souls to bodies join,
Millions will wish their lives below
Had been so short as thine."

Sacred to the Memory of Elizabeth,
daughter of Samuel & Elizabeth Ace,
who died August 17th 1829
aged ten months

Also of Elizabeth
daughter of the above
who died December 11th 1847
aged 17 years

II.

Samuel Ace 72, died 1876
"Thy will be done"

Elizabeth,
wife of the above named
died 1879, age 74
"All her sorrow left behind
And earth exchanged for heaven."

Redipuglia

for Adi, who wanted me to see this

What once had been a ramshackle
cemetery dotted with the detritus
of battle—barbed wire, battered helmets,
trenching tools, broken rifle butts—
Mussolini in his fascist grandiosity
recreated as a pristine staircase
of the dead: twenty-two giant steps,
each one-hundred-forty meters wide,
twenty feet deep, and nine feet high,
rising to the crest of Mount Sei Busi,
three giant crosses crowning all.

Twenty-one steps are faced with small
brass plates, 1900 plates per step,
each plate the name of someone dead:
   Fabio Bernardi, Terza compagnia,
      Ventunesimo battaglione del Bersaglieri,
         3rd Company, 21st Battalion of Bersaglieri;
   Mario Bottino, Sessantottesimo batteria,
      Artiglieria del mulo,
         68th Battery, Mule Artillery;
   Paolo Barbieri, Primo Reparti d'assalto;
   Ottavio Cavallo, Sardo granatieri, Gruppa Pistoia.

Behind each plate, the dead man's bones:
   Marco Esposito, Ottantatresimo compagnia
      di assistenti tecnici,
         83rd Company of Engineers;
   Allesandro Forni, Nono reggimento
      di fanteria chiara di Bersaglieri,

9th Bersaglieri Light Infantry Regiment;
Carlo Selvaggio, Quinto reggimento del Alpini;
Pietro Allegreti, Arma dei Carabinieri.

Many plates are incomplete, containing
only what could be recovered of the man:
    Luigi -----, Fusiliers;
    ----- Trovato, 28th Infantry, Pavia Brigade.

The bones and names of 40,000 dead.

The twenty-second step contains
the bones of 60,000 more
whose names were taken with their lives.

The hill contains, in all, 100,187 dead.

Across the top of every step in huge
block granite print a dozen times
and more: a single word. PRESENTE
Silent roll call of the dead:
PRESENTE   Present. We are here.

Emilio Morelli, 6th Company,
    142nd Infantry, Catanzaro Brigade;
Roberto Pappalardo, 132nd Infantry Regiment,
    Lazio Brigade, 29th Division;
Vittore Maggio, 3rd Battalion,
    58th Infantry, Abruzzi Brigade:
PRESENTE   Present. We are here.

Young men:
    Stefano Tenaglia, 14th Regiment,
        4th Bersaglieri Brigade;

Giani Caltibiano, 75th Alpino Division;
Umberto Testa, 22nd Arditi:
PRESENTE   Present. We are here.

Young men:
Cristiano Martelli, 19th Infantry, Brescia Brigade;
Battista Grassello, 48th Regiment, Ferrara Brigade;
Claudio Conti, 28th Infantry, Pavia Brigade:
PRESENTE   Present. We are here.

Young men:
Raffaello, Firenze Brigade;
Leonardo, Novara Lancers;
Gino, 52nd Alpine Infantry Division:
PRESENTE   Present. We are here.

If you stand at the base of the steps
looking up, the steps are so arranged
that all you see is the single word PRESENTE
rising out of the stone
over again, and over and over again,
marching up to the heavens,
mocking the *Duce*'s own design,
mocking the millions who come to worship here,
mocking the empty promise of salvation,
whispering, murmuring, muttering:

PRESENTE Present. We are here.

Home Before Morning

for Lynda Van Devanter (1947-2002)

If life were fair, you'd be a millionaire,
ambassador to somewhere really cool
like St. Tropez, Tahiti, or the Ritz,

maybe the Empress of Everything—
not some female Job for all the world

Almighty God just seemed to have it
in for: pass one test of faith and here's
another. And another. Yet one more.

Suffer, suffer, die. Okay, we both learned
far too young that nothing's fair in life,

that's just the way it is, there's no use
whining. And you never did complain.
Not when your lungs were so congested

that you couldn't hold a conversation.
Not when your legs swelled up so badly

that you couldn't walk a hundred feet.
Not when your joints began to fail.
Then your kidneys, too. And all the while

you just kept hoping, struggling to go on
another day, another month, another year

with Tom and Molly. How you loved
your husband and your daughter fiercely

with the burden of the knowledge of those
far too many broken boys you had to fix
and couldn't, boys too young to have the chance

to demonstrate against the war that killed them,
to be an alcoholic, to get sober,
to be an advocate for broken souls,

a witness to the worst and best we are,
to marry, make a child, write a book,

call me late at night to say you're frightened
and you need to hear another voice who's
frightened by the posturing of presidents

and statesmen who have never heard the sound
of teenaged soldiers crying for their mothers.

Great-hearted woman, may the broken boys
you tried to fix and couldn't, find you now
and guide you safely home before morning.

[Lynda Van Devanter served as a U.S. Army nurse in Vietnam in 1969-70. She was the author of the memoir Home Before Morning.*]*

Seminar on the Nature of Reality

I've never seen a person dance with death
so gracefully before. As if you were—
not rushing to embrace it, not enthralled,
but fascinated, ready to explore
this new phenomenon the way a boy
might wonder at a frog he's caught or stand,
head cocked, before a tree he thinks he'll climb.

Geez, you're dying, and you act like this is
just another challenge to be mastered.

Most of us fear death. Consider Hamlet
and his dread of something after death
so strong that we would rather fardels bear
than face the undiscovered country
from whose bourn no traveller returns.

Yet here you are, a twinkle in your eye,
telling me about the hospice music
therapist who sang for you today
and how next week you've got a physicist
coming here to lead a conversation
on what is real and what is not and how
when things are very large or very small
they don't behave the way we think they should.

You can hardly walk, you can hardly talk,
you can't even breathe without oxygen,
and still you're organizing seminars
you might not even be here to attend.

Maybe this is what you are: so large
a mind, so large a heart that you just
won't behave the way we think you should.

In Memoriam: Tom Deahl, 1930-2002

What Makes a Man

Even as my dad lay dying, cancer
back a second time and moving fast,
he blurted out, "I should have fought!"
Apropos of nothing. Out of nowhere
but the secret reservoir of memory
and shame he'd carried all his life, the weight
of it I never fully understood
until that moment. World War II, he meant.

The two of us alone: a man who'd missed
the great adventure of his generation,
Ike's Great Crusade, the crucible for all
those other men around him all his life,
the test they'd passed, the club he couldn't join;
his son, the ex-Marine, the one who'd come
back home from Vietnam insisting it was
all just bullshit, just a lethal scam
that only proves how gullible
each generation's cannon fodder is.

Only in that moment in that room
did I begin to grasp how impotent
my father must have felt through all those years,
how much he must have taken my enlistment
as a personal rebuke, and how my
subsequent insistence that I'd
validated nothing in myself
must have been to him a kind of treason.

Dying now, in 1988, he still
could not let go of Cousin Bob

who'd been dismantled by a German mine
but died a man in 1945,
not like this: wasted, helpless, haunted
by the shades of what he thought he was
and what he wished he'd been, a nurse's aide
to change his bedpan, too much time to think,
and nothing I could do to change a thing.

Letting Go

The last time I saw my mother alive,
she lay in a coma, eyes closed,
almost as if she were sleeping.

This wasn't like my father's coma
eighteen months before, him a dead man
kept alive by machines, his eyes
half-open and looking nowhere,
glazed and gray like a fish on ice.

It had taken my mom four days
to tell the doctors to pull the plug—
a wonder to me, and a lesson:
depressed, mercurial, full of rage,
burning inward like a star gone mad,
my dad was a difficult man,
and though they'd been married forty-four years,
happily married didn't apply.

Not while I'd been alive. And yet
at the end it was clear she'd never
forgotten the happy-go-lucky
guy she'd fallen in love with,
and she didn't want him to die.

And now I didn't want my mother to die.
Not that I'd wanted my father dead—
I'd long since learned to forgive what he
couldn't help—but I knew I wouldn't miss him
the way I'd miss her. She knew it too, knew

how much her sons, grown and gone and
with kids of their own, depended on her still.

She was willing herself to live
in spite of the cancer that wanted her dead.
But she looked so tired lying there,
a lifetime of sorrows and all used up,
nothing inside but a mother's love.

Alone with her, I took her hand and cried.
And then I said, "It's okay, Mom.
You've done your best. Your work is done.
It's time to rest. Let go."

An hour later she died. My aunt says
she slipped away while her pastor
was saying a prayer. Maybe just chance,
but I like to think she heard what I said
and took it to heart, and did.

The Orphan

After awhile, he gave
up waiting, rose
from beside his parents'
grave, looked once
more at the town un-
folding down below like
somebody's dream
of a perfect place
to rise above,
or leave behind,
church bells chiming
the hour of darkness,
close to home,
but home long gone.

Too long
was long enough
and longer still.

He bent to kiss the flat
brass plate that marked
his parents' grave,
said goodbye
to no one listening,
turned,
and walked away.

III. Extras

The Wreckage Along the Road

A friend from college called today.
We hadn't talked in a long time
and he wanted to reminisce. He and I
both out of place at Swarthmore College:
me a sergeant straight from the Corps,
him a workingclass kid from Cleveland
whose father had carried a union card
and lived in a rented apartment
all his life. Jeff was proud of his dad,
proud of his heritage. Even after
he'd gotten an MBA from Chicago
and started working management jobs,
he always carried the Teamsters' card
he'd had since he was a teenager
working the docks beside his dad.
"If the guys I work for knew about this,
I'd be fired," he told me once
in Memphis in nineteen seventy-nine,
pulling the card from his wallet,
"but I'm still a member. It's in my blood."
Twenty-one years have passed since then,
and today he's CEO of a firm
with manufacturing operations in China.
"I had to close the plant in Oklahoma.
The cost of labor was killing me,"
he explains, "I didn't have any choice."
Then he tells me he's going to retire
in a year or two. "I've got enough money.
I've proved myself. I'm almost fifty.
Who wants to work forever?"
I think of those workers in Oklahoma
who would like to have worked another week,
wonder if Jeff still carries his union card.

Meditations on Pedagogy

*(while listening to a presentation by
a well-paid famous Learning Expert)*

I. The Attention Controls

So many ways to waste one's time:
I am determined to shape a rhyme
by cognitive activation,
satisfaction guaranteed, salience
processing focal maintenance,
depth of detail in procession.

So many ways to waste the day:
sometimes mental effort is way
too energetically challenged,
consistently disallowing arousal,
alertness totally out of control
'til sleep be forever expunged.

So many ways to waste a life:
tempo control, a preview of self,
Monitor, Merrimac, inhibition,
facilitation of reinforcement,
systematic brain encasement
the frontal lobe of production.

What are the possible ramifications?
Energy processing mental production,
cognitive academic effectiveness
ever the interpersonal,
socially always behavioral,
domains of impacting success.

II. Levels of Language

1. Forty-four phonemes stuck in my craw,
forty-four phonemes in all;
if one of those phonemes should happen to fall,
forty-three phonemes stuck in my craw.

2. A morpheme is a small detail;
it can't really mean by itself.
But linguistic gratification would fail
if a morpheme were anything else.

3. Verbal precision
builds important networking:
college semantics.

4. Syntax, bees' wax, speckled axe, and sales tax,
brass tacks, false facts; I could use some Ex-Lax.

5. There once was a man in the Air Force
who could think of nothing but intercourse.
A woman named Val
said, "Okay, I shall—
but not without first having discourse."

6. Metalinguistics isn't just jive;
it reflects on how language works.
In generous portions it's found among high-
ly verbal learners with quirks.

7. Pragmatic influential ability;
complex, fragile applicability;
treatment-resistant vulnerability;
language of social contexts.

Artsy Fartsy, Whiskey & Girls

*on the Avenue of the Arts
Philadelphia, Pennsylvania*

There's nothing here to commend your
attention, I can tell you that
straight off, no joke, unless you're sure
what you want is only the fat

lady singing an aria
just before she drinks the poison
and dies and the whole area
from Chestnut Street down to Spruce on

Broad goes bonkers, everybody
calling out, cheering and clapping,
"Bravo! Bravo!"—and nobody
in his right mind needs that. Napping

on the railroad tracks is more fun
and probably healthier, too.
I know a place on Addison
with whiskey and girls. It'll do

in a pinch, and if this isn't
a pinch, I'd like to know what is.

All About Love

Everybody loves to hear about love,
but I don't feel like talking about that.
Gimme a break. You seen the news lately?
That missing blonde North Dakota coed
found dead in a ditch in Minnesota?
A hundred and ninety-one dead in Spain?
Thousands of pissed-off Palestinians.
Millions dying of AIDS in Africa.
Seven more soldiers dead in Fallujah—
and what are we doing there, anyway?
Where are the weapons of mass destruction?
Under a rug in a house in Peru?

Oh, don't let's talk about that, did you say?
We want to hear about love. Well okay:

I love Paris in the springtime. I love
the Broad Street Bullies and Just Saying No.
I love the way I call my bank and get
some guy in Bombay I can't understand.
I love the USA PATRIOT ACT
and having to strip to my underwear
every time I try to get on a plane.
I love a Big Mac heart attack with fries,
tax incentives for those who need 'em least,
no child left behind without a handgun
or an automatic assault rifle.

Hey, that isn't what we meant, did you say?
What did you expect? Some sentimental
Hollywood romance? Go to the movies.
Why do you think they call it Tinseltown?

Oh, Canada

Big Timber, Montana
October 2005

This paper cup I'm drinking from was made
in Canada. Ontario. Brampton,
to be exact. Now this is odd, I think:
imported paper cups. French lace, perhaps,
Dutch chocolate, Russian caviar I get.
Swiss clocks. But Canadian paper cups?
What's wrong with American paper cups?
Buy American, keep our country strong,
that's what I say. And anyway, I've been
to Canada, and I can tell you this:
it's empty. Cold. No place for anyone
but hockey players, polar bears, and seals.
Even towns with names like Medicine Hat,
Moose Jaw, Pense, and Neepawa are boring.
No mounted Mounties in their bright red coats.
No dogsleds, lumberjacks, or Eskimos.
Not, at least, that I saw, and I'd driven
thirteen hundred miles west from Winnipeg:
not a thing but wheat and elevators,
two-lane highway flat and straight enough
to hypnotize or make a sane mind crack.
I stopped just long enough to buy some beer
in Moose Jaw, turned left at Medicine Hat,
and made a beeline for yippie-eye-oh-
ki-yay-where-the-deer-and-the-antelope-
play Big Sky Country, where I find myself
today, thirty-four years down the road, eyes
full of cottonwoods, silver Yellowstone,

snow-swept Absarokas, drinking coffee
from a made-in-Canada paper cup,
amazed at how much time a man can waste
on empty thoughts and stupid diatribes.

What the Fuss Is All About

One wonders what the fuss is all about.
They say the flag is blowing in the wind.
They say the wind is blowing up a storm.
They say the moon is blue, the lies are true,
the bogeyman is here, we must believe
whatever we are told. So all for one
and one for all the money he can get
his sticky fingers on, him and all his
sticky-fingered friends. So what's new?
Just the other day, K Street three-piece-suit
walks into a bar and orders a beer.
Sorry, sir, the barkeep says, we don't serve
sleaze in here; FBI man overhears,
calls the IRS: barkeep's doing time
in Lewisburg. Let that be a lesson
to us all: Miller Lite can change your life.
Super Size me, praise the Lord, and give me
purple mountains' majesty, Hollywood
commandos, and a gas-guzzling SUV
with GPS and Power Everything.
Burn, baby, burn, some angry Black man said,
but I say what's the hurry? Soon enough
we'll burn the whole damned planet down, choke it,
strip it, starve it, melt it, pave it over,
blow it up, and bury it in empty
bottled water bottles, Pampers diapers,
plastic grocery bags, and last year's cellphones.
Then we'll see which way the wind is blowing,
whose flags are blowing in the wind, whose lies
are worth a big rat's ass, who's rich enough
to buy a one-way ticket out of Hell,
whose God is on whose side, and who's left
to wonder what the fuss was all about.

Extra! Extra!

Done before I knew it had begun.
The Yom Kippur War, that is.
I was working on a tanker out of Long Beach;
we'd been at sea for a couple of weeks,
and by the time I heard the news,
it was all over. How 'bout that,
I thought, a war come and gone and me
none the wiser—nor any the worse for wear.

That's when I began to think
the news is overrated. Most of it
is bad, in any case, and most of it
you can't do anything about
but brood. And all that paper. All those
trees. Chemicals they use to make the ink.

Life in the Neighborhood

The cop on the corner stood there and watched
while a pink rhinoceros trampled the tulips
in Mrs. Palmer's yard. "Yo!" I hollered,
"Why don't you put a stop to that?"
"Whaddaya want me to do?" the cop replied,
"Cuff 'im and run 'im in?" *Oh, swell,* I thought,
*if you want to get something done around here,
you've got to do it yourself.* So I went to the kitchen
and grabbed a bucket of cottage cheese, walked
across the street, and held it out to the rhino
—I'd read in a book that rhinos are suckers
for cottage cheese—and it worked:
he forgot all about the tulips and dug right in,
so I grabbed his horn and flipped him over my shoulder,
rolled him onto his back, and tickled the underside
of his chin till he finally fell asleep. "My hero,"
Mrs. Palmer sighed. The cop just shook his head.

IV. Epiphanies

Golfing with My Father

My father took up golf in middle age,
the dumbest game I ever tried to play,
but it was nineteen-sixty-nine, and I
was at a loss to figure out a way
to bridge the gaping generation gap
that lay between us like an open wound:

the ex-Marine just back from Vietnam
and telling anyone who'd listen what
a crock of crap the myth of manhood was;
the minister who'd spent his life convinced
his cousin Bob had died in Germany
because my dad had never been to war.

Not a lot of common ground between us
in those bad old days of Richard Nixon,
Jimi Hendrix, burning bras, and LSD.

So the afternoon my dad invited me
to play a round, I figured what the heck,
it can't be all that hard to hit a ball
that isn't moving, and it's something he
and I can do together. Which it was.

Or wasn't. More exactly, it was something
he could do while I could only hack my
way from hole to hole like some demented
backhoe operator digging random
trenches by the dozen ten and fifteen

yards apart from here to Kingdom Come.

Dad tried to coach me, but he might as well
have tried to teach a mackerel how to dance.

Before we reached the seventh hole, with what
few shreds of sanity I still had left
I realized I'd better quit before
I killed someone: my dad, or me—or maybe
the sonofabitch a hole behind us
laughing every time another chunk of God's
green acres sailed farther than the ball.

Next time my dad suggested golf, we went
for lunch to Meg & Bill's instead. They served
a wicked cheesesteak sandwich and we ate
in silence, elbows on the counter top,
shoulders hunched, our fingers dripping grease.

Breakfast with You and Emily Dickinson

for Jim Beloungy

The night Marie called home to say you'd freaked,
I almost packed my bags and headed west,
or south, or south-by-west, or who-cared-where
so long as I was miles away before
you got here with your automatic pistol
and a rage Marie had never seen before.

"Emily Dickinson, old girl," I said
to the ancient cat curled up beside me,
"you might outlast me yet." I scratched her ears
and wondered what the hell had happened,
what came loose inside your head, and what I
ought to try to do about it.
                              After all,
I knew a thing or two about loose screws,
being one myself more often than I
cared to think about.
                     That's why I couldn't
just pack up and leave. You and Marie had
given me a home when I was jobless,
thirty-one, and trying to write a book
about the war I'd fought. You'd taught me
how to pull the engine from my Beetle
when it ate a valve, strip it to the block,
and make it work again. You'd shared your love
of Pachelbel and Stan Rogers, chili
made with venison, Leinenkugel beer.
I've never known a man more generous
with time or thought, more willing to forgive

whatever pissant mood I might be in.
You and Marie just always seemed to see
the best in me. You said I made it easy,
but I know that wasn't true.
                                      And besides,
Emily Dickinson wouldn't take her
medicine from anyone but me:
I hit the road, the cat's as good as dead.

So I just sat there for the next six hours
drifting in and out of sleep all night
while you were driving down from Michigan.
A long way to drive alone. A long night
to wait alone with a grumpy old cat.

But if Emily never understood
how I always tricked her into eating
pills she hated, she never held a grudge
beyond the meal that always magically
appeared before her as the pill went down.

Sometime after dawn, I heard the front door
lock unlocking and the door swing open
and I braced myself for what might happen
next. But nothing happened next except we
looked at one another for a moment.
Then you said, "You been waiting up all night?"
"Dozing on and off," I said, "You look tired.
Want some eggs and coffee?"
                                            I might have asked
about the gun, about what should have been
just another pleasant camping trip,
but turned instead and headed for the kitchen,

suckered Emily Dickinson again,
then made a breakfast for the three of us.

Later in the day Marie got home.
I never learned what happened in the woods
of upstate Michigan that night, or how
or why or where you let the anger go.
I only know you were always a friend
I'd bet my life on. And I did. And won.

Sleeping with the Dead

I dreamed about you again last night.
This time, you were living in Tennessee,
on a horse farm, married, children
I think, it wasn't clear—you know
how dreams can be—but I finally
got you to see that I don't love you,
not like that: as if my world would end
without you in it.
                O, to have been
so close, to have shared your bed, to have
felt like I'd been raised from the dead
after all those dead I slept with
every night. It almost drove me mad
to let you go.
                But that was years ago.
You were eighteen then, and here I am
married eighteen years and sorry only
that I've never had the chance to tell you
that it's okay, that I'm okay,
that no one could have saved me then,
not you nor God, that I don't love you
anymore, but hope that someone does.

Small Talk

In the town of Freiburg, Germany,
cathedral shadows creep across the square
to where an American writer sits
admiring a scholar. "Doctor Ebel"
she had always signed her letters,
sounding just a little musty,
not vivacious, thirty-six, and unattached.
It must be nice to be a student
in a class of hers, he thinks,
wonders why she wears no wedding ring.

She asks about his wife and child.
He shows her recent photographs,
tells her how he calls them every day,
how glad he is he'll soon be going home.

"I envy you," she says, then looks away.

And then looks back and says, "One night
in World War Two, the *Luftwaffe* bombed
this town by accident. Tourist pamphlets
never mention that." Her voice a little hollow.

"You've been to war. I don't envy you for that,
but I envy you your wife and daughter,
how you wait impatiently for time
to reunite you. I was married once.
My husband left me for another woman.

"I was thinking how it must be nice
to look ahead and count the days
between you getting smaller by the hour.

"Days I count are always looking back."

Children of Adam & Eve

for Lisa Coffman

So now we're almost brother and sister,
partners, lovers, penpals of pain:
you with your Tennessee freeze-tag foot,
wrecked tendons, hobbling around on crutches;
me with my gimpy won't-be-doing-the-ten-
mile-Broad-Street-Run-this-year aching hip.

What a pair we make, traversing
together the odd terrain of the invalid,
learning at last what it means to be
Adam and Eve's descendants, kicked
out of Eden and forced to wander
a world that renews itself every spring
while you and I are ever more at odds
with our stubbornly mortal bodies.

As I write this, April daffodils;
irises, tulips, and everywhere
that iridescent yellowy green
of new deciduous leaves on trees
so vibrantly irrepressible I
don't know whether we ought to laugh or cry.

The Work of Love

for Dale Ritterbusch

Here I was in Budapest, alone
upon a bridge above the Danube
on an evening so seductive
anyone might fall in love
as easily as falling off a log,

even me: gray-haired, half-deaf,
overweight, bad eyes and all.
The falling sun suffused the air
with fire, clouds aglow, the buildings
and the river, and the whole wide sky

slowly fading into pastel pink
and pale orange of poetry and dreams.
I didn't even notice her approach
until she touched my arm and asked
if I enjoyed what I was seeing.

I said yes, then turned and saw—
how shall I explain—a woman
half my age and lovely, maybe younger,
soft as baby's breath, eyes alive
with every possibility

an aging man's imagination
could conceive: faery princess,
Magyar goddess, Eve before the Fall
until she murmured in my ear,
"You may have me, if you wish."

The Bombing of Afghanistan

for Anne

You must be sitting down to eat,
the evening air this time of day
just turning luminescent blue
and autumn crisp. I might wonder
what you've made for dinner,
how much homework Leela has,
the thousand mundane daily things
our lives are made of, and I do.
But mostly I am noticing
this moment how the stars above
the Gower shine more brightly here
than back at home: Orion's belt,
the Pleiades, the Little Dipper
pouring water into Swansea Bay.
Here it's midnight on a rare and
cloudless night in Wales, the kind
of night that poems are made of.
But though the darkness and a line
of trees hide the ruins of the Norman
castle overlooking Mumbles,
the jagged remnants of its massive
walls, the broken arches, ghostly
silence where the ring of laughter
and the might of lords once must have
seemed forever serve as stark
reminders of the transience
of what we think we wish for.
I used to wish to be a poet,
celebrated, emulated,
maybe win the Pulitzer Prize.

I've plied my trade for years, and all
it's gotten me is endless trips
too far from home, endless nights
like this, alone in strange hotels
and homes that aren't my own. Somewhere
in the darkness bombs are falling,
lives are ending in the time
it takes to write these words, and how
much time we've got together
who can know? I only know
those graceful palm trees by the hotel
pool last month in California,
the little chapel in Ohio
built in eighteen fifty-four,
that quiet Massachusetts dawn
jogging next to Walden Pond,
these stars above me, all the world
I'd give to be back home with you.

Epiphany

for Anne,
28 years later

What I remember is you at twenty-six
in the shower naked beside me,
soap cascading the length of that
heart-stopping eye-popping sight,
me like a kid in a candy shop:
most beautiful woman in all the world
and mine. All mine. All I see to this day.

V. Bodies

On the Eve of Destruction

The weekend Watts went up in flames,
we drove from Fullerton to Newport Beach
and down the coast as far as Oceanside,
four restless teenage boys three thousand miles
from home, Bob Dylan's rolling stones
in search of waves and girls and anyone
who'd buy us beer or point us toward the fun.
California. What a high. The Beach Boys,
freeways twelve lanes wide, palm trees everywhere.
And all the girls were blonde and wore bikinis.
I'd swear to that, and even if it wasn't true,
who cared? A smalltown kid from Perkasie,
I spent that whole long summer with my eyes
wide open and the world unfolding
like an open road, the toll booths closed,
service stations giving gas away.
What did riots in a Negro ghetto
have to do with me? What could cause
such savage rage? I didn't know
and didn't think about it much.
The Eve of Destruction was just a song.
Surf was up at Pendleton. The war in Vietnam
was still a sideshow half a world away,
a world that hadn't heard of Ia Drang or Tet,
James Earl Ray, Sirhan Sirhan, Black Panthers,
Spiro Agnew, Sandy Scheuer, Watergate.
We rode the waves 'til two MPs
with rifles chased us off the beach:
military land. "Fuck you!" we shouted
as we roared up Highway One, windows open,

surfboards sticking out in three directions,
thinking it was all just laughs, just kicks,
just a way to kill another weekend;
thinking we could pull this off forever.

The Bodies Beneath the Table

Hue City, 1968
(or was it Fallujah, Stalingrad, or Ur?)

The bodies beneath the table
had been lying there for days.
Long enough to obliterate their faces,
the nature of their wounds.
Or maybe whatever killed them
ruined their faces, too.
Impossible now to tell.
Only the putrefying bodies
bloated like Macy's Parade balloons,
only unrecognizable lumps on
shoulders where heads should be.

The two of them seemed to be a couple:
husband and wife, lovers perhaps,
maybe brother and sister—who
could tell—but they'd pulled the table
into a corner away from the windows,
their only protection against
the fighting raging around them,
crawled beneath it—the table, I mean—
half sitting, bent at the waist,
close together, terrified, almost
certainly terrified, nothing but noise,
only each other, only each other,
any moment their last.

All these years I've wondered
how they died. Who were they.
Who remembers.

Kosovo

The boys with pistols and shotguns
are shooting her friends in the hall.
They are shooting her friends in the library.
In her homeroom. In the cafeteria.
They are killing her friends and her teachers.

It's supposed to be just a day at school,
only another day like all of her days
in all of her schoolgirl years at Columbine.
This isn't happening. This can't be real.
At any moment, she'll awake from her dream.

But it isn't a dream. It's suburban Colorado.
Or is it Louisiana? California? Kentucky?
After awhile, it's hard to keep straight.
This could be any school in America.
This could be our own child begging for mercy.

We would like to imagine she sees an angel.
We want to imagine a merciful angel
hovers above her on fluttering wings
and lifts her forever beyond the reach
of skulls in pieces and blood-spattered walls.

But the boys with the guns don't care about angels.
The boys with the guns are settling scores.
Like Stallone and Van Damme. Like Arnold.
Destruction is power. These boys have been powerless
all of their lives. But not anymore.

When the shooting stops, fifteen people are dead,
sixteen wounded, most of them teenaged kids.
"We must teach our children," the president
solemnly says, "that violence is not the answer."
This in the week he begins the bombing of Belgrade.

September 11th

My name is Aysha Rahim.
I live in Abul Khasib
with my son Mohammed
who is helpless,
a body without a brain.

Mohammed was born in the midst
of the bombing of 1991.
He came too soon,
but I was frightened by the bombs:
night after night,
day after day;
some of them came so close.

And then my son came.
He needed an incubator and oxygen,
but we had no electricity
after the bombing began,
and my baby's brain starved.

My husband and I tried to understand.
We hated Saddam Hussein.
When your president said on the radio,
"Rise against Saddam. Now is your opportunity,"
Hassan went to Basra
and joined the rebellion.

Day after day we could see
the American planes in the air.
We knew they could see us, too.
We knew they could see

the slaughter unfolding beneath them,
but they let it go on.

In a couple of weeks it was done.
They shot my husband down like a dog.
Hassan,
and his brother,
and his three cousins,
and so many more.

I was left with Mohammed
and our older son Khalid.
Such a good boy, Khalid.
He did what he could to help.
So much to ask of a child so small,
but he never complained.

Until the day he complained
of a headache and chills.
When I put my hand to his head,
he was on fire,
as if he were burning alive
from the inside out.

I carried him all the way to the clinic.
They gave him a bed,
but they had no medicine to give him
for the fever, the diarrhea, the vomiting,
the bleeding from his anus, the delirium.
Seven days it took Khalid to die.

I have heard what happened in your country.
We have all heard, here in Abul Khasib.
How many died, did you say?

Not enough, I tell you,
not nearly enough.

But I am a patient woman.

My name is Aysha Rahim.
I live with my helpless son Mohammed
and my memories of Khalid
and my memories of Hassan.
I am going nowhere.
I can wait.

Down and Out in Darfur

What do you do when the blows keep coming?
What do you do when you're down on your knees
with your teeth kicked in and your mouth bleeding?
Where do you turn when there's nowhere to turn
and nothing and no one to turn to?

Somebody said you get up and go on.
Somebody said that you never give in,
that you turn your face to the rising sun,
that you see things through to a better end.
Somebody's always blowing smoke up your ass.

Sometimes you get to the end of your rope.
Sometimes you come to the end of the line.
Even a cat has only nine lives,
and you're not nearly so lucky as that.
You're not lucky at all. And nobody cares.

Coaching Winter Track in Time of War

The boys are running "suicides"
on the football field today:
ten-yard increments out to the fifty
and back again, push-ups in between.
It's thirty degrees, but they sweat
like it's summer in Baghdad,
curse like soldiers, swear to God
they'll see you burn in Hell.

You could fall in love with boys
like these: so earnest, so eager, so
ready to do whatever you ask, so
full of themselves and the world.

How do you tell them it's not that simple?
How do you tell them: question it all.
Question everything. Even a coach.
Even a president. How do you tell them:
ask the young dead soldiers coming home
each night in aluminum boxes
none of us is allowed to see,
an army of shades.

You tell the boys "good work" and call it a day,
stand alone in fading light while
memory's phantoms circle the track
like weary athletes running a race
without a finish line.

Manning the Walls

The day the towers came down, goggle-eyed
we stared in disbelief at death for once
so close to home we couldn't hide
our terror in the rubble of Manhattan:
complacency turned upside down and strewn
across a Pennsylvania field in burning pieces,
even Mars, our God of War, in flames.
Who'd have thought it possible? What next?

Overnight the world had changed forever,
all bets off, all the rules suspended
in the urgency to save our way of life
from lethal challenges so sinister
we need the Stars-n-Stripes in every classroom
and the FBI needs secret access
to the records of the books we're reading:
Dostoyevsky, Danielle Steele—you never
know what might be useful to a terrorist.

Well okay, I was as scared as anyone
that day, and I won't deny the world
we live in is a dangerous place.

But I remember gazing at the tiny
dot of Sputnik in the darkness
over Perkasie when I was only nine,
my country at the mercy of the Reds,
the world changed forever overnight.

I learned to Duck-n-Cover at my desk
in Mrs. Vera's room at Third Street School.
I learned to recognize the yellow signs

on public buildings reassuring us
of shelter from the Russians' atom bombs.
I learned we had a missile gap, a fail-
safe point, a hotline to the Kremlin.

That's how I grew up: Nikita Khrushchev,
Ich bin ein Berliner, Armageddon
always just a missile strike away.
One hell of a lot of good the basement
of the Bucks County Bank & Trust would do
against a thermonuclear warhead,
but anyone who tried to point this out
was either nuts, naive, or communist.

Most of us got lucky in the Cold War—
provided we ignore Korea,
Vietnam, the brushfire wars our proxies
fought around the globe for forty years,
the millions dead and maimed and dispossessed.
At least we never dropped the Big One, and
the good old USA came out on top.

No wonder our surprise on 9-11
to discover Huns outside the gates again.
Cry havoc, sound alarums, man the walls!

But any history buff can trace the rise
and fall of empires: Pax Romana,
Rule Britannia, Persia, Babylon,
Ottomans and Incas by the sword
made arrogant, and by the sword brought down.
Catastrophe is history's middle name,
and taking off our shoes in airports,

locking up librarians, inventing
threats that don't exist, I pledge allegiance
to the flag, one nation under God or not,
isn't going to save us from the Visigoths,
the Mongol hordes, Bin Laden, or ourselves.

Barbarism, communism, terrorism,
name your ism, something's always out there
in the darkness wanting in. You'd think
by now—we're talking generations here,
millennia, the whole of human time—
we'd figure out we're all in this together
and it's time to learn to share. Ask the Greeks.
Ask the Hittites. Ask the dinosaurs.

Turning Sixty

It isn't that I fear
growing older—such things as fear,
reluctance or desire
play no part at all
except as light and shadow sweep a hillside
on a Sunday afternoon,
astonishing the eye but passing on
at sunset with the land
still unchanged: the same rocks,
the same trees, tall grass gently drifting—
merely that I do not understand
how my age has come to me
or what it means.

It's almost like some small
forest creature one might find
outside the door some frosty autumn morning,
tired, lame, uncomprehending,
almost calm.
You want to stroke its fur,
pick it up, mend the leg and send it
scampering away—but something
in its eyes says, "No,
this is how I live, and how I die."
And so, a little sad, you let it be.
Later when you look,
the thing is gone.

And just like that these
sixty years have come and gone,

and I do not understand at all
why I see a gray-haired man
inside the mirror when a small
boy still lives inside this body
wondering
what causes laughter, why
nations go to war, who paints the startling
colors of the rainbow on a gray vaulted sky,
and when I will be old enough
to know.

VI. One Hand Clapping

Temple Poem

Amakusa, Japan

The sun comes up each morning in silence;
the moon disappears, but nobody sees.

Flowers dance by the roadside unnoticed;
birds twitter sweetly, but nobody hears.

People don't stop to consider what matters.
People work hard all their lives to achieve

a dream of success that will make them happy:
position or power, fortune or fame—

until they are old and they realize too late
that the beauty of living has passed them by

while the river travels alone to the ocean,
the wind sings alone in the tops of the trees.

*From the original Japanese by Shinmin Sakamura
translated by Kazunori Takenaga
and adapted by W. D. Ehrhart
at the request of Morinobu Okabe, 31st priest
of the Zen Buddhist Temple of Kokoji.*

About the Author

W. D. Ehrhart holds an Honorable Discharge from the US Marine Corps and a PhD from the University of Wales at Swansea. The recipient of the President's Medal from Veterans for Peace, a Pew Fellowship in the Arts, two Pennsylvania Council on the Arts Fellowships, a Mary Roberts Rinehart Foundation Grant, and an Excellence in the Arts Award from Vietnam Veterans of America, he is the husband of Anne and father of Leela, and teaches English and history at the Haverford School in suburban Philadelphia, Pennsylvania, where he also coaches winter track and sponsors the school's student journal of literature and art.

THE ADASTRA PRESS LIST

1979 - 2010

Zoë Anglesey, *SOMETHING MORE THAN FORCE: Poems for Guatemala, 1971-1982,* letterpress, sewn, 1982, offset 1984

Margaret Key Biggs, *PETALS FROM THE WOMANFLOWER,* ltrpr, sewn 1983

Norman R. Bissell, *STRUGGLE FOR THE DAWN,* letterpress, sewn, 1982

Martha Carlson-Bradley, *BEAST AT THE HEARTH,* letterpress, sewn, 2005

Martha Carlson-Bradley, *NEST FULL OF CRIES,* letterpress, sewn, 2000

Michael Casey, *MILLRAT,* letterpress, sewn, 1996, expanded ed., offset, 1999

Michael Casey, *RAIDING A WHOREHOUSE,* letterpress, sewn, 2004

Alan Catlin, *SHELLEY AND THE ROMANTICS,* letterpress, sewn, 1993

David Chorlton, *THE VILLAGE PAINTERS,* letterpress, sewn, 1990

Leonard J. Cirino, *THE TRUTH IS NOT REAL,* letterpress, sewn, 2006

Merritt Clifton, *FROM AN AGE OF CARS,* letterpress, sewn, 1980

Clifton, Sagan, Ehrhart, Metras, *NUCLEAR QUARTET,* folded broadsheet, letterpress, 16"x8.5" 1980

Jane Candia Coleman, *DEEP IN HIS HEART J.R. IS LAUGHING AT US,* letterpress, sewn, 1991

Jim Daniels, *NIAGARA FALLS,* letterpress, sewn, 1994, offset, perf. 1995

Jim Daniels, *DIGGER'S BLUES,* letterpress, sewn, 2002

Jim Daniels, *DIGGER'S TERRITORY,* letterpress, sewn, 1989

Cortney Davis, *THE BODY FLUTE,* letterpress, sewn, 1994

Gregory Dunne, *HOME TEST,* letterpress, sewn 2009

W.D. Ehrhart, *BEAUTIFUL WRECKAGE: New & Selected Poems,* offset, 1999

W.D. Ehrhart, *GIFTS,* broadsheet, letterpress, 9"x 12", 2003

W.D. Ehrhart, *MATTERS OF THE HEART,* letterpress, sewn, 1981

W.D. Ehrhart, *MOSTLY NOTHING HAPPENS,* letterpress, sewn, 1996

W.D. Ehrhart, *THE OUTER BANKS & Other Poems,* letterpress, sewn, 1984, offset, perfect bound, 1984

W.D. Ehrhart, *THE DISTANCE WE TRAVEL,* letterpress, sewn, 1993, offset, perf. bound, 1994

W.D. Ehrhart, *SLEEPING WITH THE DEAD,* letterpress, sewn, 2006

W.D. Ehrhart, *WINTER BELLS,* letterpress, sewn, 1988

W.D. Ehrhart, *THE BODIES BENEATH THE TABLE,* offset, perf. 2010

Jim Finnegan, *MY ANGELS,* broadsheet, letterpress, art by Susan Finnegan, 8.75" x 11.75", 1995

David Giannini, *ANTONIO & CLARA,* letterpress, sewn, 1990

David Giannini, *AZ TWO: Words of Travel,* letterpress, sewn, 2009

David Giannini, *From ELLIPSES, PART II,* broadsheet, ltrpr, 8.75"x 11.75", 1996

Jack Gilbert, *GOING WRONG,* broadsheet, letterpress, 8.75 x 11.5", 1992

D M Gordon, *FOURTH WORLD,* letterpress, sewn, 2010

Andy Gunderson, *CITY PAUSES,* letterpress, sewn, 1980

Gertrude Halstead, *memories   like burrs,* letterpress, sewn, 2006, offset, sewn, 2006

Linda Lee Harper, *BLUE FLUTE,* letterpress, sewn, 1999

Dawnell Harrison, *VOYAGES,* letterpress, sewn, 2010

Michael Hettich, *BEHIND OUR MEMORIES,* letterpress, sewn, 2003

Harry Humes, *ROBBING THE PILLARS,* letterpress, sewn, 1984

Geoffrey Jacques, *SUSPENDED KNOWLEDGE,* letterpress, sewn, 1998

Greg Joly, *HAND LABOR,* letterpress, sewn, 1992

Greg Joly, *VILLAGE LIMITS,* letterpress, sewn, 2008

Richard Jones, *INNOCENT THINGS,* letterpress, sewn, 1985

Richard Jones, *SONNETS,* letterpress, sewn, 1990

Richard Jones, *THE STONE IT LIVES ON,* letterpress, sewn, 2000

Richard Jones, *WINDOWS AND WALLS,* letterpress, sewn, 1982

Anna Kirwan, *THE FIRST THING,* letterpress, sewn, 2001

Joseph Langland, *TWELVE POEMS with Preludes and Postludes,* letterpress, sewn, 1988, offset, perf. bound, 1989

M.L. Liebler, *BREAKING THE VOODOO,* letterpress, sewn, 2001

Christopher Locke, *HOW TO BURN,* letterpress, sewn, 1995

Thomas Lux, *A BOAT IN THE FOREST,* letterpress, sewn, 1992

Thomas Lux, *PECKED TO DEATH BY SWANS,* letterpress, sewn, 1993

Thomas Lux, *THE BLIND SWIMMER: Selected Early Poems, 1970-1975,* offset, perfect bound, 1996

Thomas Lux, *THE DROWNED RIVER,* offset., perf. bound, reprint, 1993

D. Roger Martin, *NO DREAMS FOR SALE,* letterpress, sewn, 1983

Dawn McDuffie, *CARMINA DETROIT,* letterpress, sewn, 2006

Louis McKee, trans., *MARGINALIA: Poems from the O ld Irish,* bilingual, letterpress, sewn, 2008

Gary Metras, *DESTINY'S CALENDAR,* offset, perf. bound, reprint, 1988

Gary Metras, *SEAGULL BEACH,* letterpress, sewn, 1995

Gary Metras, ed., *THE ADASTRA READER,* offset, perfect bound, 1987

Gary Metras, *THE NECESSITIES,* letterpress, sewn, 1979

Gary Metras, *THE NIGHT WATCHES,* letterpress, sewn, 1981

Michael Miller, *EACH DAY,* letterpress, sewn, 2005

Judith Neeld, *SEA FIRE,* letterpress, sewn, 1987

Ed Ochester, *ALLEGHENY,* letterpress, sewn, 1995

Ed Ochester, *COOKING IN KEY WEST,* letterpress, sewn, 2000

Ed Ochester, *THE REPUBLIC OF LIES,* letterpress, sewn, 2007

Peter Oresick, *OTHER LIVES,* letterpress, sewn, 1985, offset, perf. 1985

Stephen Philbrick, *THREE,* letterpress, sewn, 2003

Stephen Philbrick, *UP TO THE ELBOW,* letterpress, sewn, 1997

Constance Pierce, *PHILIPPE AT HIS BATH,* letterpress, sewn, 1983

David Raffeld, *INTO THE WORLD OF MEN,* letterpress, sewn, 1997

David Raffeld, *THE BALLAD OF HARMONICA GEORGE and Other Poems,* letterpress, sewn, 1989

Michael Rattee, *FALLING OFF THE BICYCLE FOREVER,* offset, 2010

Michael Rattee, *MENTIONING DREAMS,* letterpress, sewn, 1985

Michael & Kiev Rattee, *ENOUGH SAID: A Poetic Dialogue Between Father & Son,* letterpress, sewn, 2002

Susan Edwards Richmond, *BOTO,* letterpress, sewn, 2002

Susan Edwards Richmond, *PURGATORY CHASM,* letterpress, sewn, 2007

Karen Rigby, *FESTIVAL BONE,* letterpress, sewn, 2004

Becky Rodia, *ANOTHER FIRE,* letterpress, sewn, 1997

Miriam Sagan, *ACEQUIA MADRE: Through the Mother Ditch,* ltrpr, sewn, 1988

Miriam Sagan, *POCAHONTAS DISCOVERS AMERICA,* ltrpr, sewn, 1993

Charles Scott, *OLD ORDNANCE,* letterpress, sewn, 2005

Tom Sexton, *A CLOCK WITH NO HANDS,* offset, perf. bound, 2007

Tom Sexton, *LEAVING FOR A YEAR,* letterpress, sewn, 1998

Tom Sexton, *THE LOWELL POEMS,* letterpress, sewn, 2005

Laurel Speer, *DON'T DRESS YOUR CAT IN AN APRON,* ltrpr, sewn, 1981

Barry Sternlieb, *FISSION,* letterpress, sewn, 1986

Wally Swist, *ACCOMPANIMENT,* broadsheet, letterpress, 8.5" x 11", 2003

Wally Swist, *FOR THE DANCE,* letterpress, sewn, 1991

Wally Swist, *WAKING UP THE DUCKS,* letterpress, sewn, 1987

Susan Terris, *POETIC LICENSE,* letterpress, sewn, 2004

Emmet Van Driesche, *THE LAND BEFORE US: Poems of the Sea,* letterpress, sewn, 2004

Mary Jane White, trans., Marina Tsvetaeva's *NEW YEAR'S: An Elegy for Rilke,* letterpress, sewn 2007

Clarence Wolfshohl, *SEASON OF MANGOS,* letterpress, sewn, 2009